EASTER PR
for the church

cible

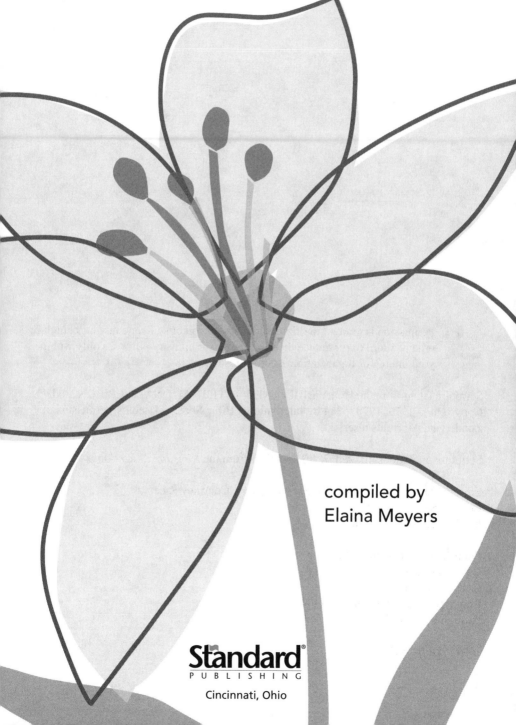

compiled by
Elaina Meyers

Standard
P U B L I S H I N G
Cincinnati, Ohio

Editorial team: Dawn A. Medill, Elaina Meyers, Courtney Rice
Cover design: Brigid Naglich
Inside design: Bob Korth

Published by Standard Publishing
Cincinnati, Ohio
www.standardpub.com

ISBN 978-0-7847-2351-7

Contents

READINGS

Good-bye Is Not Forever

MARSHA CHUDY

Summary: HEATHER misses her grandmother, who died almost a year ago, and doesn't know how she will be able to celebrate Easter now that her grandmother is gone.

Characters:
HEATHER—teenage girl
JOSH—teenage boy, HEATHER's brother
DARCIE—teenage girl, HEATHER's friend

Setting: family kitchen

Props: table with two chairs, two bowls and spoons, cereal box, milk carton, three backpacks (one for each of the characters), schoolbook (in Josh's backpack), facial tissue (in Heather's pocket)

Running Time: 5 minutes

SCENE 1

JOSH is sitting at the table eating breakfast. HEATHER enters and places her backpack on the floor next to the table.

JOSH: *[looks up at her]* You've been crying again, haven't you?
HEATHER: *[nods]* I miss Grandma so much. I wish she hadn't died. *[sits down and pours cereal into her bowl]*
JOSH: Crying about it all the time isn't going to bring her back.
HEATHER: *[glares at him]* I know that. But Easter won't be the same without her. Who will make the Easter bread?
JOSH: You and Mom will have to do it.
HEATHER: But Grandma's bread was special. No one can make it the way she did. *[shoves her bowl away and gets up]* You don't even care, do you? You must not have loved Grandma very much. *[She grabs her backpack and exits.]*

[Josh picks up the dishes, cereal box, and milk and carries them off the stage.]

Scene 2

HEATHER and DARCIE enter the kitchen and stand there talking. They are both wearing backpacks.

DARCIE: What are you doing for Easter?

HEATHER: Grandpa's coming over, and we're having dinner at home. *[sighs]* I wish we could skip Easter.

DARCIE: Why? You love Easter.

HEATHER: That was before Grandma died. I don't feel much like celebrating anymore. It's always been a family tradition to go to her house.

DARCIE: Sometimes you have to make new traditions.

HEATHER: I don't want new traditions. I want things to be just the way they always were.

DARCIE: The other kids are talking about you.

HEATHER: What are they saying?

DARCIE: They know you're a Christian, and they see how upset you are about your grandmother's death. They don't understand why you're taking it so hard if you really believe that she went to Heaven and that you'll see her again. You do believe that, don't you?

HEATHER: *[frowns]* I used to. Now I'm not sure what I believe. Listen, can we just drop the subject?

DARCIE: *[ignores HEATHER and continues talking]* You act as if you're the only one who cared about your grandmother, but you're not. Your brother cared, and your parents too. It must be hard for your mom to have to prepare for Easter all by herself this year.

HEATHER: You don't know what it's like—both of your grandmothers are still alive. Besides, I told you I don't want to talk about it anymore. Maybe you should go home.

[DARCIE exits first, then HEATHER]

Good-bye Is Not Forever

Scene 3

Josh enters carrying his backpack. He pulls a schoolbook out of it, sits down, and begins to study. There is an empty chair at the table. After a few moments, Heather enters.

HEATHER: Do you have a few minutes? I want to ask you something.

JOSH: Sure. What's on your mind?

HEATHER: *[sits down]* Do you miss Grandma?

JOSH: Of course I do.

HEATHER: Then why do you act like you don't?

JOSH: What do you mean?

HEATHER: You go out with your friends . . . you laugh about things. You don't seem to care at all that she died. *[starts to cry]*

JOSH: I do care. In fact, I miss her a lot. Do you really think Grandma would want us to mope around and never enjoy ourselves again? You know she wouldn't. She loved life, but she was looking forward to being with Jesus.

[Heather takes a tissue out of her pocket and wipes her tears.]

Josh: When I start to feel bad because Grandma's gone, I remind myself that I'll see her in Heaven some day.

Heather: Do you really believe that you'll see her again?

Josh: Of course. Grandma believed it too. Don't you?

Heather: *[thinks about his question for a few moments]* Yeah, I do. I guess I just miss her so much that I forget I'll see her again. *[She stands up.]*

Josh: Feel better now?

Heather: *[nods]* Yeah. I'm going to offer to help Mom get ready for Easter. I want her to teach me how to make Grandma's special bread.

Josh: I think Grandma would have liked that.

The Living Bread

IRIS GRAY DOWLING

Summary: AMIR, the boy who shared his lunch with Jesus, returns home to tell his mother about meeting Jesus. He wants her to meet Him too. Three READERS make applications about the story.

Characters:
MAMA—AMIR's mother
AMIR—the boy who gave his lunch to Jesus
3 READERS

Setting: a simple room from Bible times
Scene 1—AMIR tells his mama what happened when he met Jesus
Scene 2—Readers' Theater

Props: Persian rugs, stool, workbench, water pot, dough, rolling pin
Six pictures to be projected on the screen near the stage, as follows:
1. children of Israel gathering manna in the wilderness
2. baby Jesus in the manger in Bethlehem
3. Jesus on the cross
4. Last Supper—Jesus with the disciples
5. a large open Bible showing John 6—"The Bread of Life"
6. a picture of the resurrected Jesus with caption: "I am the Bread of Life"

Running Time: 15 minutes

Music for choir: "Break Thou the Bread of Life" verses 1, 2, and 3; and "People Need the Lord" verses 1 and 2. See the optional ending to this song that uses "He is the bread of life" as the last phrase for each verse. (Songs can be found in *Hymnal for Worship & Celebration,* Word Music.)

Scripture References: Exodus 16; John 6; Luke 22:19; 1 Corinthians 11:24

Costumes: plain or striped gowns with colored sashes, head wrappings, sandals

MAMA is kneading dough; AMIR is heard singing backstage.

AMIR: *[enters, excited]* Mama!
MAMA: AMIR, where have you been?
AMIR: *[anxious to talk]* You'll never guess what happened today!
MAMA: Did you eat the lunch I packed for you?
AMIR: That's what I want to tell you!
MAMA: You ate it, didn't you?
AMIR: Mama, I shared it.
MAMA: What are you talking about? It was only enough for one person. You didn't eat it if you shared it.
AMIR: *[moves his hands to show excitement]* The lunch you packed for me was so good that more than 5,000 other people liked it and ate it!
MAMA: *[doubts AMIR]* What kind of story did you think up this time? Let's talk about who really ate your lunch.
AMIR: I'm not joking, Mama. There was a man out on the hillside near town. He was teaching a crowd of people. They came from far away and listened to Him for three days.
MAMA: Didn't they bring food with them? Did you think you could share your little lunch with so many hungry people?
AMIR: I don't know, I guess they didn't bring enough for three days. Two men who knew the teacher asked if anyone in the crowd had any food. I thought I could share a part of my lunch with the teacher.
MAMA: Didn't you realize that if you didn't eat you might faint in the heat and wouldn't have strength to get home?
AMIR: Yes, I told them I only had a little lunch to share. They quickly took me to Jesus, the teacher. He looked at me so kindly as He put His hand on my shoulder.
MAMA: *[sighing]* Then I guess you didn't eat what I packed, did you?
AMIR: Mama, that's the miracle I'm trying to tell you about!
MAMA: A miracle?
AMIR: Oh, Yes, Mama. This teacher told all the people to sit down. *[lifts hands toward Heaven]* He looked up to Heaven and gave thanks to God for my lunch. Then He started breaking the loaves into little pieces and told His helpers to pass them out to the people.
MAMA: Really, son. They must have been little tiny pieces.
AMIR: That's what's so amazing! He kept breaking, and breaking, and breaking, and little pieces just kept coming.

Mama: Are you sure that's not another one of your made-up stories?

Amir: No, Mama, I had plenty to eat and so did all those thousands of people.

Mama: Now I know your imagination is running wild!

Amir: You might not believe me, but the people were all full and no one went away hungry.

Mama: Impossible!

Amir: Impossible for us, Mama, but not for Jesus.

Mama: That just sounds like another of your big stories!

Amir: It *is* a big story! Jesus is a special person!

Mama: He had to be to feed all those people. Did you say there were more than 5,000?

Amir: Yes. Everyone ate all they wanted and when His helpers gathered up the crumbs they had 12 full baskets.

Mama: Hmmm . . . *[Mama shakes her head.]* It sounds like He is a miracle worker!

Amir: Yes, Mama. I heard one of His helpers say, "Jesus is the Christ, the Son of God." Then I heard the one named Andrew say, "He is the bread of life." *[pause]* I've been wondering what they meant.

Mama: I need to see Him to believe what you're saying.

Amir: *[moves toward his mama]* Will you go with me to find Him?

Mama: I'm sure He's not going to feed all those people every day.

The Living Bread

AMIR: No, not with bread loaves, but with the bread of Heaven. Jesus said if people would believe in Him, the bread of life, they would never get hungry.

MAMA: *[shows attention]* That is a different message. I wish we didn't get hungry.

AMIR: Yes. I heard Jesus tell the people that they have to believe He is true bread from Heaven and that He gives eternal life to those who believe and follow Him.

MAMA: Well, when I was at the market I heard some people talking. The

The Living Bread

owners weren't too happy when no one came to buy food. I guess people didn't come because they were filled up with your lunch.

AMIR: Oh, Mama! *[laughing]* That is a gigantic miracle, isn't it? I wish you had been there to see it. While I was there I also heard how Jesus healed some sick people. He even made a blind man see! I will never forget how Jesus looked at me with such kind eyes.

MAMA: All right, Amir, We'll go tomorrow. Right now I need to make more loaves for our food.

AMIR: I can't wait to see Jesus again. *[looks to audience and thinks aloud]* He said it was His Father's will that everyone would believe and have eternal life.

MAMA: I don't understand that message, but it sounds important. I'd like to hear more about eternal bread and eternal life.

AMIR: Another thing I heard Jesus say is that He would have to die, but would rise again in three days and people would see Him alive before He would go back to His Father in Heaven.

MAMA: *[looks inquisitive and interested]* What else did He say?

AMIR: He said, "Blessed are you who believe in me because you see me and see the things I do, but more blessed will be many who believe in me when they don't see me."

MAMA: Why will they believe in what they can't see?

AMIR: Well, Jesus pointed to Himself and said, "I am the Way, the Truth, and the Life; *[points to Heaven]* no one can come to my Father in Heaven if they don't believe in me."

MAMA: I do want to see this teacher for myself. We will go tomorrow. Now it's time for you to rest from a long day.

AMIR: May I take a little loaf of bread for Jesus tomorrow?

MAMA: *[shakes head]* We'll take enough to share with Him.

AMIR: *[rests on rug]* All right, Mama, I love you! *[lights out as music plays]*

Choir sings "Break Thou the Bread of Life" verses 1, 2, and 3.

Scene 2: Readers' Theater

[Three READERS stand left, middle, and right on stage. Project each picture as listed. See detailed list under props.]

READER 1: *[Project picture #1—manna]* Exodus 16 tells how God fed the people of Israel with manna in the wilderness. He provided it every day for many years. It had to be picked up fresh each day and could not be saved for the next. They had to believe and obey what God said to have the good life-giving manna.

READER 2: *[Project picture # 2—nativity]* Jesus was born in Bethlehem, which means "House of Bread". Jesus is the fulfillment of that life giving manna. He showed people who He is. In John 6, He broke bread to give to people. *[Project #3—cross]* He also told them He would have to die and His body would be broken for our sins. Some believed but some did not understand what he was saying.

READER 3: When Jesus gave thanks and broke the bread, it was not the last time. *[Project #4—last supper]* In Matthew 26, Jesus celebrated the Passover meal with His disciples. He gave thanks and broke the bread to share with them. He tried to help them understand that He had to die on the cross or there would be no forgiveness for their sins. Through His burial and resurrection they could receive eternal life.

READER 1: Jesus also wants us to believe and accept the forgiveness of sin He offers because of His death on the cross.

READER 2: Remember how Jesus broke bread with His disciples at the last supper? We are His disciples if we believe and accept His forgiveness. How fitting that He said of the bread, "This is my body given for you; do this in remembrance of me. As often as you eat this bread and drink this cup, you show the Lord's death until He comes."

READER 3: *[Project picture #5—open Bible]* We also need to spend time with God to gain spiritual strength for each day. Just as the Israelites gathered the manna daily, we need to get some of the bread of life each day by reading His Word—the Bible.

ALL READERS: *[Project picture #6—risen Christ]* Only Jesus, the living bread, can satisfy a hungry soul.

Choir sings "People Need the Lord" verses 1 and 2.

The Upper Room

CYNTHIA G. ROEMER

Summary: The disciples are in an upper room following Jesus' crucifixion. They are despondent and confused over what has taken place, until a shocking chain of events renews their hope and gives them a vision for the future.

Characters:
PETER—disciple of Jesus
ANDREW—disciple of Jesus
JAMES—disciple of Jesus
JOHN—disciple of Jesus
PHILIP—disciple of Jesus
MATTHEW—disciple of Jesus
FIVE OTHER DISCIPLES
MARY MAGDALENE—follower of Jesus
JOANNA
OTHER MARY
CLEOPAS—follower of Jesus
NIGEL
JESUS

Setting: an upper room in Jerusalem, three days after Christ's crucifixion

Props: first century room setting with door that opens; first century clothing; spotlight/special lighting; low table; wooden bowls, plates, and cups; white strips of cloth; beach setting; firewood; fake fire; fake fish; dramatic background music (optional)

Running time: 15 minutes

Scene 1

An upper room where the eleven disciples are gathered

JAMES: *[pacing angrily back and forth]* What are we doing sitting around in a locked room? Is this where the past three years have brought us? Is this how it's going to end?

JOHN: Calm down, brother. We have endured a crushing blow. Jesus *was* our last three years. Now He is gone. We need time. Time to think; time to heal.

MATTHEW: *[bitterly]* If it wasn't for Judas this would not have happened. That traitorous fiend!

ANDREW: *[solemnly]* Judas has paid for his crime with his life . . . and his soul.

PETER: *[in quiet reflection]* Judas is not alone in his guilt. I sent Jesus to the cross as well. Three times I denied I even knew our Lord . . . after proclaiming I was ready to die for Him! I will never forget the look of disappointment in His eyes.

JOHN: *[placing a hand on Peter's shoulder]* We all let Him down. We allowed fear for our own lives to cloud our faith.

PHILIP: What amazes me is how willingly He gave himself over to them. It was as if He knew they were coming for Him. Like He was almost expecting it. *[A sudden knock on the door draws their attention. Peter rises and slowly approaches the door. Before he can speak, a woman's voice sounds outside it.]*

MARY MAGDALENE: Open the door. It's Mary! *[Peter looks around at the other disciples in surprise then unlocks and opens the door.]*

MARY MAGDALENE: *[face beaming with joy and emotion]* Praise God! Jesus is alive! *[The disciples stare at each other, bewildered]*

JOANNA: *[excitedly stepping up beside Mary]* It's true. With our own eyes we have witnessed angels of light inside the empty tomb of our Lord!

MARY MAGDALENE: Jesus told us that He was to be crucified and on the third day rise again. And so He has! *[The disciples begin to murmur to each other with questions and disbelief.]*

JOHN: *[to the women]* But that is impossible! I stood at the foot of the cross and watched Him die!

PETER: There must be some mistake. It cannot be as you say.

MATTHEW: Do not add to our sorrow by telling us fantasies and wishful thinking.

MARY MAGDALENE: *[with sternness in her voice]* Go then, and see for yourself if our words are indeed fantasies or truth! The tomb is empty, and our Lord lives! *[Peter glances around then bolts out the door.]*

Scene 2

The disciples are standing and reclining around the table, looking troubled. Peter has returned from the tomb and holds strips of cloth in his hands.

JAMES: What do you make of it, Peter? Do you think someone has taken Him away?

PETER: *[looking at the clothes dejectedly]* I don't know what to think. The stone was sealed and guards were posted; that much I know. Yet, as the women said, Jesus is not there.

JOHN: *[hopefully]* Perhaps the women spoke the truth. Jesus did many miraculous things. He brought Lazarus back to life. Why couldn't He come back to life too?

PHILIP: But how could a dead man bring himself back to life?

ANDREW: Nothing makes sense any more. *[A loud knock sounds at the door.]*

PETER: *[nervously]* Who's there?

CLEOPAS: *[excitedly]* Cleopas and Nigel! We bring good news! *[Peter opens the door, and the two excited men hurry in]*

JOHN: Tell us. What news have you?

CLEOPAS: Jesus has risen! We have walked with Him and even dined with Him!

PETER: *[in disbelief]* What?

NIGEL: It *is* true. He walked with us on the road to Emmaus. Our hearts burned within us as He explained the Scriptures.

CLEOPAS: Still, He looked different to us. We did not recognize who He was until He broke bread and gave thanks.

JAMES: Then where is He?

NIGEL: Gone. He vanished as quickly as He appeared. It was as if…*[lights turn off, then brighten quickly; Jesus appears in the room]*

JESUS: Peace be with you. *[The disciples fall back in fear]*

JESUS: Do not fear. It is I.

JOHN: *[still fearful]* But how can it be? I watched you die! With my own eyes I watched them lay your body in the tomb!

JAMES: It is His ghost!

JESUS: Why do you doubt? Can't the maker of Heaven and Earth bring life

where there is no life? *[holding out blood-stained hands]* Look at my hands and feet. Feel the wound in my side. *[The disciples edge closer, still unsure.]*

JESUS: Have you anything to eat? *[Andrew hands Jesus a piece of fish and He eats it. The disciples draw closer, finally believing.]*

PETER: *[falling at Jesus' feet]* Master! It is You! *[The other disciples gather closer and begin worshiping and praising God.]*

Scene 3

The disciples are with Jesus on a beach, seated around a fire, and eating fish. Peter and Andrew walk toward the rest and join them at the fire.

ANDREW: *[excitedly]* What a catch you gave us, Lord! One hundred fifty-three fish in all, as I counted.

PETER: They nearly busted our nets!

JESUS: *[smiling, then looking at the ground more somberly]* Peter, do you love me?

PETER: *[sincerely]* Yes, Lord. You know that I do.

JESUS: Then feed my lambs. *[There is a long pause before Jesus speaks again.]*

JESUS: Simon Peter, do you truly love me?

PETER: *[more earnestly]* Yes, Lord. You know I do.

JESUS: Take care of my sheep. *[another long pause]*

JESUS: *[gazing intently at Peter]* Do you love me, Peter?

PETER: *[with sadness and urgency in his voice]* Lord, You know everything. You know that I love You!

JESUS: Feed my sheep. Truly, when you were young you went and did as you pleased. But when you are old, you will stretch out your hands and be taken where you do not wish to go.

PETER: *[with understanding]* I failed You once, Lord. I will not fail You again. *[lights off suddenly]*.

JESUS: *[speaking loudly]* "Therefore go and make disciples of all nations, baptizing them in the name of the Father and of the Son and of the Holy Spirit, and teaching them to obey everything I have commanded you. And surely I am with you always, to the very end of the age."

Optional ending: spotlight Jesus before He says His last line and play dramatic music in the background.

Return to Gethsemane

DIANA C. DERRINGER

Summary: JOHN reflects on his shortcomings surrounding the crucifixion of Jesus.

Character:
JOHN—an apostle

Setting: the garden of Gethsemane

Props: Bible times costume, large stone, greenery

Running Time: 2 minutes

JOHN sits on a stone at the edge of the garden.

Sit here, watch, and pray. That shouldn't be so hard, should it? *[sorrowfully]* But we didn't do it—none of us. During one of the most heart wrenching times of Jesus' life, we all let Him down.

Jesus led me, along with Peter and James, to an area in the garden just a stone's throw from where He prayed. Even if He had never told us, the sorrow and distress He felt was obvious. When He fell on His face before the Father, my heart broke. His sweat was like drops of blood, and *[emphasize feelings of desire]* I wanted to support Him in prayer. I wanted to ward off temptation, *[pause]* but I couldn't. I was tired and my eyelids felt so heavy.

When He saw that we slept, He must have been so disappointed. He knew our desire to be faithful, but our weakness prevailed. Finally, His struggle over, He told us to rise; His time of betrayal had arrived. Even as He spoke, Judas brought a crowd armed with swords and clubs to arrest Jesus. *[speaking with anger and disappointment]* How could Judas betray Him with a kiss? *[hesitate briefly]* How could the rest of us run like cowards who had never experienced His holy presence? We did not watch. We did not pray. *[voice catching]* We slept and then we ran! *[long pause]*

But, praise God, our relationship didn't end there. Jesus forgave us. Even as He suffered on the cross, He showed and spoke forgiveness. Not just for me but for all people. And such a short time after my display of fear and irresponsibility, He entrusted me with the care of His own mother! *[pause]*

With His death, our faith faltered again and we questioned His role as Messiah. *[Shake head in disgust.]* How could we continue to be so weak? For the victory of the cross was temporary; *[mounting excitement]* He arose from the dead, and so much that He tried to explain before became abundantly clear. Through His death we can have life. By dying for our sin and weakness, He offers forgiveness and an inheritance in Heaven. I failed Him, but He will never fail me. What a promise!

Through His Mother's Eyes

CAROL S. REDD

Summary: An Easter story that looks through MARY's eyes as she watches her Son go from a baby to the cross.

Characters:
MARY—mother of Jesus; non-speaking role
TODDLER JESUS—non-speaking role
BOY JESUS—12-year-old boy; non-speaking role
JESUS—non-speaking role
RELIGIOUS LEADERS—non-speaking roles
BLIND MAN—non-speaking role
LITTLE CHILDREN—non-speaking roles
SOLOIST—sings "Mary Did You Know" throughout the entire presentation

Setting: This drama plays out in various scenes across the front of the auditorium and across the stage.

Set: Front of the auditorium is empty. Benches are placed at front left side of stage and cross is at back center stage. The container of theatrical blood is placed at base of cross so it cannot be seen by the audience.

Props: large white cloth bundled to look like a swaddled baby Jesus, benches, cross, theatrical blood (in open, flat container), Bible times costumes

Running Time: 10 minutes

SOLOIST begins singing, "Mary Did You Know." MARY slowly enters from the back and walks down the center aisle, carrying baby JESUS. She stops at center front of auditorium (not yet on stage) and turns to face the audience.

MARY raises her face toward Heaven as if thanking God for baby JESUS. She moves her mouth and appears to be talking to God, but makes no sounds. Just then the cloth drops from her arms as she continues to hold onto a corner of the fabric. She looks startled because her baby is gone. MARY frantically looks around as if she doesn't know what to do.

While all eyes are on MARY as she anxiously searches for her baby, TODDLER JESUS quietly appears on the right front of the auditorium.

Suddenly MARY sees TODDLER JESUS as He waves His arms around trying to get her attention. He appears to be calling, "Mom! Mom!" but does so silently.

MARY clutches the fabric to her as she hurries to TODDLER JESUS. She silently talks to Him and hugs Him and it is obvious that they are very happy together. MARY then looks toward Heaven as if thanking God for her toddler. Mary moves her mouth and appears to be talking to God, but makes no sounds.

While she is looking up and talking to God, TODDLER JESUS slips away and remains out of sight.

When MARY looks back to where TODDLER JESUS was, she realizes He has disappeared and once again is startled. She frantically looks around as if she doesn't know what to do.

While all eyes are on MARY as she anxiously searches for TODDLER JESUS, the BOY JESUS quietly stands before the RELIGIOUS LEADERS who are seated on the benches at front left of stage. He appears to be teaching them. He silently mouths words and uses hand movements as the religious leaders nod in agreement to Him and to each other.

Suddenly MARY sees BOY JESUS. Still clutching the cloth, she moves toward Him and watches intently for approximately 10-15 seconds. She then lifts her hands upward to thank God for JESUS once again. As she is doing this, the BOY JESUS and the RELIGIOUS LEADERS slip away and remain out of sight.

When MARY looks back she realizes JESUS has once again disappeared and she is hysterical.

Then the man JESUS slowly begins to walk toward the BLIND MAN who is sitting on the front center stage floor.
Suddenly MARY (still clutching the cloth) sees JESUS and moves toward Him as she reaches out to Him and silently watches as He heals the BLIND MAN. JESUS then walks over to the LITTLE CHILDREN who are sitting on the floor nearby. The LITTLE CHILDREN all raise their faces to look up at Him and smile. JESUS appears to speak silently to each of them as He pats them on their shoulders, holds their hands, or places His hand on their heads.

Through His Mother's Eyes

After about 10-15 seconds of watching JESUS with the LITTLE CHILDREN, MARY lifts her hands upward to thank God for her Son, JESUS. But as she is doing this, JESUS, the BLIND MAN, and the LITTLE CHILDREN slip away and remain out of sight.

When MARY looks back she realizes JESUS has once again disappeared and she is frantic.

Suddenly, MARY sees the empty cross. She very slowly walks toward the cross as she clutches the cloth to her heart. MARY slowly kneels down in front of the cross as if sobbing.

While kneeling, MARY discretely presses her white cloth in the pan of theatrical blood at the base of the cross.

MARY slowly stands and as her heart appears to be breaking, she holds the blood-stained cloth out in front of her (in easy view of the audience), and exits the auditorium.

From the Manger to the Cross

DIANA C. DERRINGER

Summary: SPEAKER compares and contrasts the stories of Christmas and Easter.

Character:
SPEAKER

Setting: any location

Props: a cross on one side, a baby or doll in a manger on the other side

Running Time: about 2 minutes

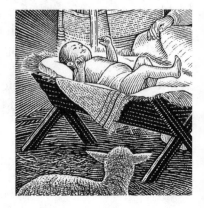

SPEAKER stands at center stage, directing attention toward the manger when speaking of Christmas (the first statement in each paragraph) and toward the cross when recalling Easter scenes (the remainder of the paragraph).

During Christmas we sing of baby Jesus sleeping on the hay. Easter brings to mind the reason that baby came.

We recall the triumphant message: Have no fear because of God's good news. Later, Jesus warns his closest followers of betrayal and deceit.

A choir of angels declares God's glory and proclaims peace. God's chosen one, whose birth the angels made known, announces His coming death.

Shepherds worshipped an infant in a stable. Soldiers arrest Him, now grown, as He prays in a garden.

A bright star shining in a clear open sky becomes replaced with a night of denial, grief, and lies.

Wise men followed a star searching for the promised one. Those with power found Him, beat and spit on Him, and mocked Him with a scarlet robe and crown of thorns.

The baby was held and loved in His mother's arms; the man hung to die on a cross.

Camels carried gifts from faraway lands for the growing child. A sponge filled with wine vinegar was offered to the dying man while those beneath the cross gambled for His clothes.

The child grew to live a sinless life. His lifeless body was then placed in another man's tomb.

The manger could not detain the babe; the cross could not defeat the man.

Finish by reading the following Scriptures: Luke 2:6, 7; 23:33; 24:1-8.

From the Manger to the Cross

The Blacksmith's Spikes

DIANA C. DERRINGER

Summary: The BLACKSMITH who made the spikes used for Jesus' crucifixion bemoans his unintentional role.

Characters:
BLACKSMITH
SMALL BOY—son of the BLACKSMITH

Setting: a blacksmith's shop in Jerusalem

Props: Bible times costumes, large block of wood with a spike on it, blacksmith's hammer, a basket filled with spikes

Running Time: 1 minute

The BLACKSMITH, holding his hammer and picking up a spike from the block of wood, gazes at it intently and shakes his head before speaking. The SMALL BOY, with a non-speaking role, holds a basket of spikes and watches the BLACKSMITH closely.

How hard to imagine that an item this small can cause so much pain. Last Friday when the soldiers stopped for more spikes I knew another crucifixion must be planned. *[shaking head in disbelief]* Little did I realize their intention to kill our Savior. My heart aches with the knowledge that, although unintended, something I made shared a role in His torture and death. My nails pierced His flesh; my nails held Him on that cross. *[looking down and speaking slowly]* And it was for my sins that He died. *[looking up]* With every spike I make, I remember His suffering for me *[pausing, then extending hand with spike forward]* and for you. Please take one as you leave so you too will remember.

[After the service, have people stationed at each entrance to hand out nails.]

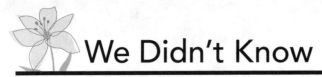

We Didn't Know

KAREN M. LEET

Lord, we didn't know You would come this way. Meek and mild, quiet, and sometimes hardly noticed. We didn't know You would come to walk among us. We didn't know You would walk at all. We expected a warrior king; a king on horseback; a king with a sword of fire and power.

We expected a warrior but you came as a shepherd, gathering us together, calling us to follow, carrying a shepherd's crook and not a sword. You came to show the way, to lead if we would follow, to teach with gentle stories that could pierce our hearts if we let them.

We expected riot and rebellion. We expected an overthrow of governments and conquerors. We expected loud rhetoric. But you came speaking softly, touching our hearts. You came telling us to give Caesar what belonged to him and to God what was His. You came speaking obedience instead of revolt. Yes, you overturned tables in the temple, but mostly you wanted to overturn hearts.

We didn't know You would wear away shoe leather as You stepped through our lives. We thought You would ride in majesty, leaving us humbled at the sight of You. Instead You washed feet and took last place and spoke with kindness and love. You came as the sacrificial lamb, the Lamb of God, the only one willing to die for us, for our sins.

You came to bring us freedom, yes, but not from tyrannical governments or harsh rulers. Instead you promised us true freedom, freedom from the inside out, freedom from the punishments we deserved for our sinful behaviors. Instead of leading attacks, You led us into hope and faith. Instead of raising a banner of rebellion, You promised us eternal life. Instead of lifting a sword against the enemies, You urged us to forgive those who hurt us.

We didn't know You would come this way, to walk among us, to speak softly but with tremendous authority. We didn't know. We knew You would bring signs and wonders. But we didn't know You would ask us not to spread the news. It didn't matter if we tried not to tell. Crowds thronged you anyway. Their hearts stirred at the sight of You.

We didn't know You, Lord. We didn't understand what You taught us. We didn't see why You had come and what God's plan might be. We didn't know You would come for a purpose we never expected. You came to die. We didn't want You to leave us. We would have kept you here with us. We would have fought for You, but that was not what You wanted. We didn't understand and so we ran for cover, hid and trembled, grieved for the loss of You. We denied You and betrayed You and failed You. We could not even stay awake with You in the garden, in Your pain.

We didn't know what it meant, Your dying. We couldn't understand. We were shocked and terrified, lost and confused, bereft and abandoned.

We didn't know then what it all meant. But You showed us, didn't You, Lord? You came back to us. You walked among us again. You spoke to us, with love and reassurances. You showed Yourself to us and helped us understand God's purpose through it all.

You died for us, then and now and always. You gave your precious life for us, to pay for our sins. You made Yourself a living sacrifice—for us. You died on a cross. For us!

And now we know, Lamb of God, good shepherd, Savior, king of kings, and Lord of lords.

We know too that next time You come, You *will* come as the lion of Judah, our warrior king.

Poems

JESUS' BIRTH, LIFE, DEATH, BURIAL, AND RESURRECTION

The Wood Story
S. Bruce Harrison

He was born in a wooden manger
crudely built by an unknown stranger.
There He let out His first cry.
Could He know He was born to die?

Many a home He may have made,
building from wood was His trade.
And yet He never owned a home,
along the shores of Galilee to roam.

Captured among the olive trees,
kissed by a traitor, Jesus was seized.
Sentenced to die on a wooden cross,
it was for us He suffered such loss.

Paradise Regained
Douglas Raymond Rose

Three men were crucified today
on Calvary's mound of sod;
one a thief, the other a robber,
and one the Son of God.

The robber asked for repentance
as his sins his conscience did prod;
"Today you'll be with me in Paradise,"
said the Sovereign Son of God.

Jesus' Hands
Crystal Bowman

With His hands He healed the sick,
the helpless and the weak.
He touched blind eyes so they could see,
and tongues so they could speak.

With open hands and open arms,
He let the children come.
He laid His hands upon their heads
and blessed each precious one.

With His hands he broke the bread
and poured a glass of wine.
He shared a special supper
with His helpers one more time.

With His hands nailed to a cross
and with His arms stretched wide,
He took our sins upon Himself.
He suffered and He died.

But death could not contain our Lord.
His purpose was to save.
With nail-scarred hands He rose again
and left an empty grave.

Jesus blessed His faithful friends
before He said good-bye.
With lifted hands toward Heaven,
He rose into the sky.

So let us lift our hands to Him
and praise Him as we sing.
Jesus is the Lord of Lords,
our Savior and our king.

Rolled Away
Crystal Bowman

Jesus hung upon a cross
His friends stood near and cried.
"It is finished!" Jesus said.
He hung His head and died.

He paid the debt for all our sins.
He died for you and me,
so we can be forgiven
and we can be set free.

Then Jesus rose up from the dead—
the stone was rolled away!
He conquered death and conquered Hell.
He is alive today!

Jesus is our hope and peace.
He heals our pain and strife.
To all who put their trust in Him
He gives eternal life.

So on this Easter Sunday—
rejoice! Be glad today!
Our Savior lives forever.
The stone's been rolled away.

The Glory of Easter
Dolores Steger

There's the glory of Easter
when Jesus was tried,
sacrificed on the cross
where, tormented, He died.
Buried in a cave
that was torn open wide,
arose resurrected,
to sit by God's side.

Echoes of Morning
Susan Sundwall

Their Master in his dying throes
had torn their world asunder.
But from the horror of His death
the disciples woke to splendor.

The creeping dawn revealed the tomb
that could no longer hold Him.
He'd burst the bounds of time and space,
revealed Himself unto them.

What awesome joy they must have felt
at the center of their being.
Their hearts and minds were stupefied
at what they all were seeing.

Go and tell! Go and tell!
soon echoed through the morning.
And lilies from the fields of Heaven
were now His cross adorning.

The fire of the truth they told
keeps burning through the ages.
And we will add our witness
to the store of history's pages.

The Fisherman
Dolores Steger

The Fisherman stands on the shore,
He beckons souls; their spirits soar.

They recognize Him, for they see
the one who's come from Galilee.

They've seen Him hailed with palms and cheers,
and crucified, as they shed tears.

For us all on the cross He died.
So casts He now His net so wide.

He's risen from a stone-cold grave,
to fish again for more to save.

Two Believers
Amy Houts

As two walked to Emmaus
from Jerusalem,
the man who died to save us,
Jesus, walked with them.

The two who walked with Jesus
thought military might
the power that would save us,
not suffering and plight.

Giving thanks, they broke bread,
drinking from the cup.
"He is no longer dead!"
Their eyes were opened up.

Returning to Jerusalem,
to the eleven men,
the two believers told them,
"It's true. The Lord has risen!"

Jesus is the Savior.
Jesus is the way.
Blessed king, Redeemer.
Rejoice on Easter Day!

The Traveler
Dolores Steger

Who is that Traveler there in the road?
He looks so familiar to me.
I'll walk in His footsteps; I'll follow Him close.
Should I ask Him just who He might be?

He's turning; He's smiling; He's waving me, "Come."
And then in that moment I know
it's Jesus, my Savior, arisen, who lives!
And wherever He goes I will go.

Poems

SPRING AND GOD'S CREATION

Pre-Easter Communion
Douglas Raymond Rose

I love to get up extra early,
before the break of Easter Day,
to enjoy Communion with my Father
as He softly lights the dawning way.
The sun becomes my chandelier,
the sky my stained-glass art.
My pew is cushioned greening grass;
a sparrow sings hymns from God's heart.
My bread is to do the Father's will;
my sweet wine the morning dew.
If I listen closely I can almost hear
Christ saying, "I arose for you."

Welcome
Dolores Steger

Welcome the flower a-bloom in the field,
welcome the birds soaring high.
Welcome the sun brightly shining above
and the gentle white clouds passing by.

Welcome this morning now, rise up with joy.
Welcome this Easter; it's here.
Welcome with praise and rejoicing, that's it,
the most wonderful day of the year.

A Resurrection Song
Douglas Raymond Rose

Blossoms and birdsong
in the golden rhythm of spring.
It's Easter resurrection time—
and my happy heart sings.

Merry marigolds and daffodils
hugging hillside streams.
It's Easter resurrection time,
and my happy soul sings.

Lilies
Dolores Steger

When lilies all appear in bloom,
my thoughts move toward an upper room.

When lilies, bright, then catch my eye,
I hear the crowd's Hosanna cry.

When lilies, white and pure, I see,
a hill, a cross, seem clear to me.

When lilies all appear in bloom,
rejoice, it's there, the empty tomb.

Joy
Dolores Steger

Each colored egg and chocolate bunny
may make Easter bright and sunny;
but Easter's joy you'll truly find,
when "resurrection" comes to mind.

Spring Is in the Air
Dolores Steger

When sunny skies and breezes soft
seem to be everywhere,
you know with such a certainty
that spring is in the air.

When flowers bloom and birds take wing
and days are bright and fair,
you cannot help but tell yourself
that spring is in the air.

When of a cross, and empty tomb
you're suddenly aware,
you know the resurrection's true
and Easter's in the air.

The Signs of Springtime
Alan Cliburn

I love the signs of springtime,
like birds singing in the air,
the sound of children laughing—
God's presence everywhere.

I love the scent of lilacs
blooming by the lane.
I love the warmth of sunshine,
I love the gentle rain.

But most of all it's Easter
that makes my heart to sing,
and resurrection Sunday
happens every spring!

Poems

WHAT THE RESURRECTION MEANS

I Wonder
Alan Cliburn

I wonder how I would've felt
if they nailed me to that tree.
I'm sure it would've hurt inside
to hear the mockery.

If I came down from Heaven above
to save all who believe,
why would they sentence me to death
and make my mother grieve?

If I had been a healer
of so many who lay ill,
no doubt in anger I'd react,
regardless of God's will.

But praise the Lord it wasn't me
who went to Calvary.
Instead it was the Son of God
who died to set me free.

That was on a Friday
when they placed Him in the tomb.
But on Sunday all who looked
saw just an empty room.

I wonder how it must've felt
to conquer death and sin.
I only know that due to Him
Christ Jesus lives within.

He is alive! Hallelujah!
And I don't have to wonder about that!

Rejoice Before the Lord Your God
Based on Deuteronomy 12:18
Lorena E. Worlein

Rejoice before the Lord your God
in everything you do.
For Christ has risen from the dead
and makes each day anew.

Rejoice before the Lord your God
in everything you say.
Sing forth the glories of His name
each and every day.

Rejoice before the Lord your God
with body, heart, and soul.
For He has power over sin
and makes each spirit whole.

Rejoice before the Lord your God
for all that He has done.
He is our glorious conqueror.
The victory He has won!

He Asked a Question
Karen M. Leet

"Do you love me?" He asked.
"Well, do you?"
And I wondered, "Do I?
Do I love Him?"
I thought of all He'd done
for me—for love of me.
He'd left a home in Heaven,
a place of peace and beauty,
to live here with me,
to teach me and help me,
to lead me and guide me,
to watch over me, and protect me.
He left a perfect place
to walk with me,
by my side through
all life's troubles.
And if that wasn't enough,
He died for me too,
on a cross in bloody agony.
He died, then rose again
for me—to give me life
everlasting, eternal, forever
with the Father.
And thinking of all this,
I fall to my knees and say,
"Yes, Lord, yes, I love You."

My Blood Is Shed for You
Karen M. Leet

In a dream I saw His face,
His eyes full of compassion
for me, while I was lost
in my own selfish will,
in my sin and separation from God,
in my stubborn resistance,
in my pain and confusion.
Lost—not knowing which
way to go or how or why.

In a dream I saw His hands,
bloody nail prints in each,
reaching for me, urging me
to come to Him, to give
Him my fears, my worries, my doubts.

In a dream I heard His voice
calling, calling me—"Come to me,
come, just come and I will care for you,"
and He told me, "My blood
is shed for you. I died
for you, and I would do it all
again, in a heartbeat. For you.
Come, just come to me."

An Easter Wind
Douglas Raymond Rose

Perhaps a gentle wind blew that day
outside the empty Garden tomb,
when Christ arose that Easter morn
as ivory lilies burst into bloom.

Perhaps a gentle wind may blow today
as I watch the Easter sunrise dawn,
as I remember Christ is alive and well
this Resurrection morn.

He is Risen!